CREATIVE HOME DESIGN

KITCHENS AND DINING ROOMS

NONIE NIESEWAND

Stoddart

First published in 1987 by
Stoddart Publishing Co. Limited
34 Lesmill Road
Toronto, Canada
M3B 2T6

Reprinted 1995

Published in Great Britain by
Conran Octopus Limited
37 Shelton Street
Covent Garden
London WC2H 9HN

Canadian Cataloguing in Publication Data

Niesewand, Nonie
    Kitchens and dining rooms

(Creative home design)
ISBN 0-7737-5736-8

1. Kitchens. 2. Dining rooms. 3. Interior
decoration. I. Title. II. Series.

NK2117.D5N53 1987   747.7'6   C87-094032-5

Printed and bound in Hong Kong

CONTENTS

KITCHENS

Your dream kitchen may be a romantic vision in a rustic farmhouse with flagstone floors, herbs hanging from wooden beams, a smell of baking coming from an old iron range and a bustle of people round a large pine table. If you are a creative cook, it may be an ultra-modern, stainless steel kitchen designed for a professional chef with the very latest gadgetry and every utensil and convenience available. Alternatively you may prefer a narrow, ship-shape galley, with all clutter concealed in laminated fitted units and the digital clock on the micro-wave giving a countdown for a meal in minutes.

Obviously the reality is rather different. A reasonable budget will rarely stretch to the ultimate dream kitchen. Space is also a severe limitation since you cannot fit a large, airy, country-style kitchen into the average home. Yet, whatever shape or size you have available, and no matter how small your budget, the lay-out, the style and the atmosphere of your kitchen are for you to decide and the possibilities are almost endless. There is no single, universal kitchen lay-out which is right for everyone.

The lay-out must be carefully planned to accommodate the wide range of things which make up the kitchen – bulky equipment such as cookers, storage for everything from frozen meat to those fondue skewers you occasionally use, gadgets and appliances, and probably a place for the family to eat. The lay-out must also take account of power and water supplies, safety, comfort and efficiency.

The style of your kitchen is something only you can decide. The choices are enormous. You must decide on the type of storage units and major fittings you want. You must choose the finish for your surfaces – it could be plastic laminate, natural wood or a subtle paint effect – and when you have made that decision you must decide on the precise colour or pattern. The type of floor you decide on will not only affect cost and efficiency but also style.

The atmosphere of your kitchen will come from the personal details and final touches you give to it, but it is something to keep in mind from the outset. We rarely have the opportunity to build a kitchen from scratch, so this book will help you deal with styles and lay-outs you inherit as well as offering a complete guide to creating the kitchen of your dreams.

PLANNING CHECKLIST

- What do you dislike about your present kitchen?
- How many adults, children and pets will be using the room?
- What activities will the kitchen be used for?
  - cooking
  - laundry
  - home office
  - dining
  - ironing
  - sewing
- Which meals do you eat or serve in the kitchen?
- What are the storage requirements?
- Which appliances do you require?
  - refrigerator
  - microwave oven
  - fume extractor
  - cool larder
  - washing machine
  - freezer
  - oven
  - hob
  - dishwasher
  - tumble drier
- Do any appliances require special plumbing or ducting?
- Where will you put the rubbish?
- How many electric power outlets will you need for appliances, and where should these be sited?
- Will all working areas have adequate lighting?
- Are your kitchen requirements likely to change over time?
- What sort of atmosphere would you like to create?

In this bold, small-space kitchen, everyday necessities are treated as objects of interest in their own right. The angular black fume extractor hood is both practical and good-looking and an array of utensils decorates the wall.

These two views of the same small kitchen before and after decoration show that redesigning a kitchen does not need to be expensive, or to involve major structural changes, in order to be extremely effective.

1 *Before refurbishment, the kitchen was fairly typical of the kind often inherited in housing built or redecorated on a speculative basis in recent decades. The imitation timber doors of the kitchen units, tile-effect flooring and roller blinds are the cheap fitments of the modern townhouse kitchen. Worse, the arrangement of kitchen units and appliances has not been designed to overcome space limitations. The unfortunate placement of the old gas stove, which juts awkwardly into the room, creates a dead, wasted corner space. The dog basket tucked away below is ready to trip up the cook moving from the stovetop with a saucepan full of boiling liquid, and the coffee maker stashed in the corner of the worktop is virtually inaccessible. The display unit for spices and coffee mugs, which might make sense in a larger kitchen, takes up a lot of valuable wall space to store very little. With such limited storage space, appliances and gadgets occupy the worktop area, and some items are stored in inaccessible spots on top of tall wall units.*

1

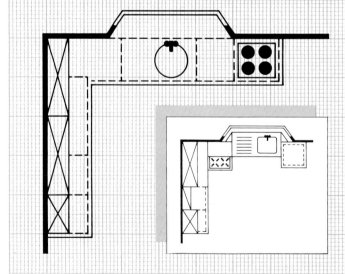

2

2 *This inexpensive but successful transformation is achieved by replacing the kitchen units and the stove. The new design also reinforces the modern style of the room, rather than working against it. To successfully transform the inherent style of a room is always more expensive. Functional self-assembly kitchen units such as those used here are easy to find in a wide variety of shapes, sizes and styles.*

Kitchen units with cool grey melamine-faced doors and smart 'D'-handles have been fitted according to an ergonomic plan which provides maximum storage – even in the corner – and ample worktop space for preparing food, while minimizing walkabouts between the stove and the sink. No space-wasting spice racks interrupt the block of wall units. Narrow-slatted grey Venetian blinds admit the natural light necessary for a window sill herb garden even as they provide privacy and enhance the clean lines of the large window – the room's best feature. By night, the sink and food preparation area is illuminated by downlighters recessed into the top of the window bay.

The white vinyl flooring with fine diagonal stripes, the white plinths of the floor units and the white melamine countertops with their white-tiled splashback all contrive to make this kitchen more spacious.

These two kitchens illustrate the way a single modular system of manufactured kitchen units can be used to different effect in different spaces. With a range of units which offers many options, from the usual floor and wall units to finishing touches like space-filling shelves and plinths, it is possible to put together a customized kitchen that suits the individual requirements of a room and its occupants.

1 The owner of this small, working kitchen has chosen units with white laminate surfaces and beech edges and handles for a clean, sharp look. Open, easy-access adjustable shelves instead of closed wall cupboards display decorative storage jars and tableware. Everything is stored within arm's reach for the busy cook and, although it is all on view, the result is a warm and welcoming workplace, rather than a cluttered mess. Cupboard doors hide unsightly bulky items at a lower level, and the floor unit plinths, which are usually no more than a decorative kickboard panel, have been heightened and deepened to house drawers and trays for storing infrequently used items. This range of kitchen cupboards includes appliances – a stove and a refrigerator – which fit snugly into built-in units.

1

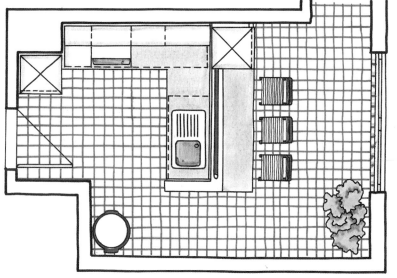

2

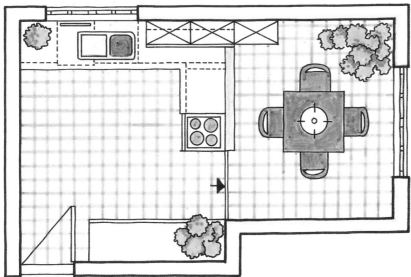

2 *In this slightly larger kitchen/ dining area, the same kitchen units – recognizable by their distinctive handles, drawer fronts and deep storage plinths – are used to different effect. Here, banding with primary colours in parallel stripes – an easy way to brighten a kitchen and make appliances more fun – begins on the free-standing stove and refrigerator, and goes on to provide a strong visual link between cooking and dining areas on the ceiling. There are many ways in which changes in surface finish detail can be used to introduce colour or revamp old units. Drawer handles, rails, peel-off adhesive colour strips and coloured tile grout are a few of the many ideas for improving a kitchen without replacing the units. Both the kitchen and dining areas of the room feature large, many-paned windows with louvred shutters outside and use houseplants to focus attention on them, against the natural looking background of easy-care doors faced with beech-effect laminate to match the beech trim. Open display shelves enliven a corner of the dining area and one corner beneath the long white countertop. This lay-out accommodates free-standing appliances and makes good use of the modular kitchen system, which includes the neat shelf below the wall cupboards.*

1 *Small, narrow galley kitchens pose a challenge. There is the obvious problem of how to accommodate all the required appliances, as well as sufficient work space for food preparation and cooking, and storage for ingredients and utensils. Safety is another consideration: saucepan handles projecting past the edge of the stove top are especially dangerous when floor space is cramped.*
This long, narrow kitchen is dominated by the off-centre positioning of the window at the far end. A food preparation area has been created along one wall, where a deep countertop houses a built-in stove. To make the room seem as light and spacious as possible, everything is white. Lights under the wall cupboards cast light on the worktop.

2 *A very basic kitchen can be fitted in a space not much bigger than a walk-in cupboard. Here, inexpensive self-assembly kitchen units with white melamine doors have been teamed with white worktops, walls, tiles and grid-patterned flooring to make this tiny, windowless kitchen as light as possible. Bright blue 'D' handles anchor a blue and yellow colour scheme introduced by small details, from the blue wall socket to the collection of yellow plastic sink accessories.*

1

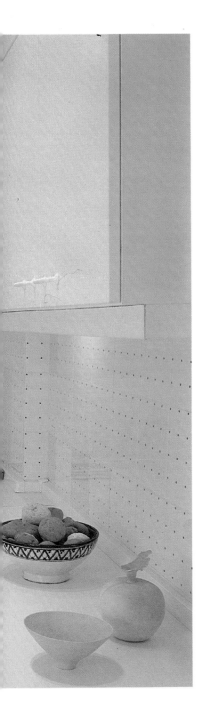

3 *This imaginative treatment unboxes a basic box of a kitchen. Curved open shelving and a curved worktop at one end of the room add much-needed interest. White tiles, which unify the overall scheme, are laid in an unusual and effective stepped pattern to form a splashback against the painted concrete block wall. Carved and painted shelf brackets are as decorative as the storage containers and utensils they display. Two large skylights in the slanting, lean-to roof of this tiny extension ensure plenty of light.*

4 *Long, narrow white tiles highlighted by black grout improve the proportions of this difficult room. Laid horizontally across the floor, they visually widen the narrow room; the rhythm of vertical tiles along the side walls seems to shorten the distance to the far wall, making the room seem more square than rectangular. Even the pattern of the latticed diamond-pane windows contributes to the effect by drawing the end of the room forward. Double sinks fitted in the very small work area below the window have an oval shape which complements the geometric regularity of the tiled surfaces. As in so many small kitchens, plain white units have been chosen to avoid a dark, cramped effect.*

Medium-sized kitchens offer more scope for adopting a preferred lay-out than small ones, where planning is often a question of making the most of a kitchen along a single wall or at best a narrow galley kitchen with units lining opposite walls. When planning a kitchen for a medium-sized rectangular room, consider a U-shaped plan, especially for an open-plan room with a kitchen area. An L-shaped kitchen plan also works well if the kitchen is combined with a dining area.

1 *One end of this graciously proportioned room has become a kitchen, partitioned from the rest by a built-in peninsular counter that houses the cooker top. Below, glazed cabinets and open shelves stocked with attractive tableware face into the living/dining area. A counter along the wall opposite the U-shaped work area ends in a similar open-shelf unit, with a curved edge to make a swift entrance into the kitchen from the adjacent door a great deal easier. The high ceiling permits a tall column unit to house a double oven.*

2 *This workmanlike kitchen is basically designed along an ergonomic L-shaped plan which minimizes walking to and fro between the stove, sink and refrigerator. A narrower counter tucked into a wall alcove extends the worktop to make a U-shaped area.*

1

2

3

3 *Where there is enough space, and a large enough budget, an island unit in the middle of the room adds extra work and storage space. The high, pitched ceiling of this A-frame house provides an interesting shape for a spacious kitchen. The generous floor space is broken by a long island work station in the centre whose marble worktop, with access from both sides, allows the cook to enlist several helpers. There is a desirable change of levels in the work surface which is difficult to achieve except with an island unit. The worktop around a sink should be about 75mm (3in) higher than the usual work surface to allow for reaching down into the sink. Heavy tasks which employ the back and arm muscles, such as kneading bread, are best carried out at a slightly lower level.*

On the far wall, a tall built-in structure includes cupboards for brooms, ironing board and the hot water tank, along with open alcoves designed to house a double oven and a large refrigerator/freezer. Plenty of space has been allowed to encompass the opening of doors. A stainless steel stove top is sited close to the oven to avoid carrying cooked dishes a long distance to brown or grill in the oven. Appliances which require plumbing are lined up along the outer wall of the room, with access to water inlet and outlet pipes.

The farmhouse-style kitchen is most often associated with a big kitchen: a large old-fashioned iron stove throwing out steady warmth, a huge central table that doubles as work space for baking, a dresser that displays blue and white china and a low window sill, with a cat asleep beside the geraniums. So often the kitchens built in modern houses are small, or, at best, medium-sized and they may share space with the living room or dining room. It is rare to find a big kitchen furnished with modern laminates and technologically advanced appliances. The three examples illustrated here are planned to incorporate modern labour-saving innovations, but still present comforting charm.

1 *This large kitchen revolves around a central island work station with a cooker top and chopping board. A wine rack and a rubbish bin with a bottom-hung door flap are built into one side of the island unit. One side of the kitchen houses a refrigerator and a freezer, each hidden behind a burnished metal door framed with black.*
The same black outlining technique highlights the unscreened narrow window, making it a feature of the far wall. Since it is the outer wall, the washing machine, dishwasher and sink are plumbed in there.

1

2

3

2 *A square kitchen of ample dimensions is given a fairly conventional treatment with a U-shaped work area defined by the units lining three walls, and a dining table area in the foreground. The cast-iron cookware upon the worktop is at hand for use in the double oven. A double refrigerator and separate freezer are housed in special units away from the warmth of the oven.*

3 *As the concept of the fitted kitchen has become dominant, with its emphasis on long, unbroken worktops, it is easy to forget that kitchen tables provide useful work surfaces. They have the advantage of doubling up for casual dining once the meal is cooked. This scrubbed pine farmhouse table, bleached over its years of use as an additional worktop surface, has an impressive array of cook's equipment suspended within an arm's reach. With its turned-up, tray-like edge, the counter is clearly not intended as a food preparation area. Every detail contributes to the quaintly old-fashioned air of this kitchen: the Delft-style tiles of the splashback, the white-painted tongue-and-groove boards, the dark wooden worktop with its unusual edge, even the brass hinges and handles. Nonetheless, the modern kitchen equipment – the large stove and the refrigerator – are perfectly at home.*

Cooking equipment is the most fundamental part of the kitchen – the very reason for its existence. So your kitchen plan – and style – will be influenced by the type of cooker you need and the placing of the appliance. The kitchen where a commuter cook speedily thaws and heats pre-cooked convenience foods in a microwave is different in every way from the kitchen where a cast-iron cooking range is steadily warm all day and used to cook the produce from a country garden. Country kitchen or hi-tech streamline, these labels are determined as much by the oven you choose in the first place as by the fittings in which food and equipment are housed. Today, the latest technology does not necessarily mean a space-age design. Behind dark enamelled fronts with brass towel rails there could be an ultra-modern fan oven which cooks faster at lower temperatures. Even the timer that allows you to cook at your convenience does not have to be a digital design but could be a traditional Roman numeral clock face that fits perfectly into an old-style wood kitchen.

Never has the cook had more choice. Eye-level appliances can now combine hot air ovens or conventional convection ovens with an adjoining microwave and a grill. One hob fitting can include both electric and gas rings with an adjoining deep fryer, charcoal barbecue or warming plate. Separate ovens and hobs can be slotted into a fitted kitchen so that they merge completely with the overall design. Ceramic hobs can be as little as 30mm (1in) in depth and be powered by tungsten light elements, called halogen heat, which produce a bright glow of light but are as efficient and easily adjustable as old-fashioned gas burners.

Alternatively, your preference may be a free-standing cooker which is available with many of the latest innovations in oven settings, timers and with eye-level grills and revolving spits. Microwave ovens can be built into a kitchen wall unit or can be added to an existing kitchen as a free-standing unit which sits on the worktop or a trolley. There is a wide variety of other countertop cooking appliances to supplement or upgrade traditional large appliances: coffee-makers, toasters, sandwich/waffle-makers, electric woks and frying pans, rice steamers, slow cooking pots with timers, portable ovens and grills, deep-fat fryers.

Air and fume extractors are also available in an enormous range of styles and sophistication – from the basic wall extractor fan to ultra-modern, slimline hoods on push-button control or ornamental extractor hoods chosen to complement your kitchen style.

Before you choose your appliances visit every available display of kitchens and appliances so that you can judge not only the best type of cooker but how it looks in a kitchen setting. Consider if it is practical for your kitchen in terms of size, style and, most important, the way you cook.

This very professional cook's kitchen is designed so that a busy chef can produce vast quantities of food with the minimum of fuss or clutter. Gadgets, pots, pans and utensils line every available surface, ready to be put to work: kettle, food processor, coffee-maker, waffle-maker, bread-slicer, scales. Open, easy-access shelves line the room so that no one need rummage frantically through the cupboards.

At the heart of this working kitchen – the central island work station – everything is at hand to keep the cook from dashing to and fro. There is ample worktop space around the built-in cooker top. An enormous fume extraction hood is designed to remove the significant amount of steam and vapour generated in a large, active kitchen. The extraction unit is covered with a wire grid which provides a handy storage place for skillets and ladles within arm's reach of the cooking area. A pair of large double ovens are easily accessible from the island work station.

How do you cook? Not so long ago you had to choose between gas or electricity, but today appliances are designed to cook with both. You can buy a stove with both electric and gas burners or a double oven with an electric unit below and a microwave or gas oven above. Perhaps you prefer to cook on a large, old-fashioned, cast-iron stove which burns wood or coal. Modern models of traditional stoves can also be oil- or gas-fired.

The most striking change introduced by advanced kitchen planning has been the separation of the stove top from the oven. The newest hobs are ultra-slim, 30mm (1¼in) deep, so that an appliance can be fitted beneath. Microchip technology has revolutionized the way ovens and burners work, too. For example, an electrosensor ceramic cooking surface – so flat that it fits firmly into the worktop – can bring a saucepan of liquid to the boil, then the heat can be instantly reduced to a pre-selected simmering temperature and maintained exactly.

1   *Here, a pair of double gas burners have been set into a custom-built low-level recess in the marble worktop of an island counter. Varying the levels for different tasks is attractive as well as practical. A fume extraction hood above removes steam and cooking odours.*

1

2

3

4

2 *Here, a combination of three independent panels chosen from a matching range form a customized, versatile cooking area in a small-space kitchen. Gas burners have long had certain advantages over regular electric ones: cooking rings heat up almost instantly, their temperature can be finely adjusted to the exact cooking heat required and the heat cuts off as soon as the burner is turned off, which is especially useful in a kitchen with limited counter space. In this kitchen a double gas ring sits beside a panel with two electric burners, which are best for economic cooking where an even heat is more important than accurate cooking temperature. The third panel is a deep-fat fryer with a stainless steel lid that doubles as a hot plate.*
Other types of panel are available, such as barbecue grills or rotisserie spits with efficient fume extractors built in.

3 *The electric burners of this inset cooking area are virtually flush with the surrounding worktop, an ideal arrangement for a cook who works at the stove.*

4 *Certain ceramic glass stove tops have tungsten tubc burners which produce a special kind of light –sometimes called 'halogen heat' – that responds to temperature adjustments instantly, like a gas burner.*

1 *The oven you choose from the immense variety available will determine — and depend on — the kind of food you serve and the sort of kitchen you plan. If you know that your stay in the house is to be a short one, you may prefer to have a familiar free-standing stove that incorporates both cooker top and oven which you can take with you when you move. These can be quite simple or very elaborate, with double ovens, built-in grills and storage areas for pots and pans. Separate, built-in ovens, on the other hand, blend in with the kitchen units and can be sited wherever it is most convenient, preferably at waist height or above to avoid bending over to lift heavy pans. Built-in ovens can also fit into a small space. Kitchens with island or peninsular units are often designed so that gregarious cooks are not isolated from family or guests while they work. A free-standing stove, which must have its back to the wall, would defeat this purpose. The solution adopted here is ideal: a cooker top is dropped into the work surface of the island unit and an independent split-level oven is sited along a nearby wall as close to the stove as possible. Double ovens often combine two or more types of appliances for maximum flexibility: often a conventional oven below, supplemented by a fast-cooking microwave above.*

1

COUNTERTOP COOKING

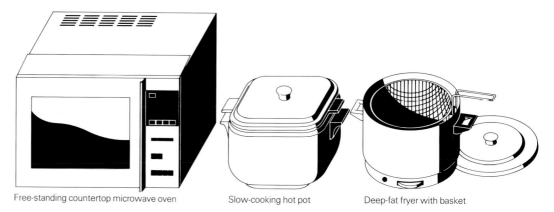

Free-standing countertop microwave oven   Slow-cooking hot pot   Deep-fat fryer with basket

2

3

2 Older farmhouse and cottage kitchens may retain their original wood- or coal-burning cast-iron stoves which may also heat the hot water supply. A handsome modern version, such as the one illustrated here, comes with a bright enamel finish which is easy to clean, and is fuelled by oil or natural gas, not solid fuel. It also requires a great deal of space, a sound floor that will bear its considerable weight and a big kitchen, since it throws out a lot of heat.

3 In many kitchens, the conventional free-standing stove, with cooker top above and oven below, remains the best option. This kitchen combines the ergonomic advantages of a conventional stove with the clean look of a built-in unit.

4 You can update a kitchen by adding any of a number of small appliances which sit on the countertop.

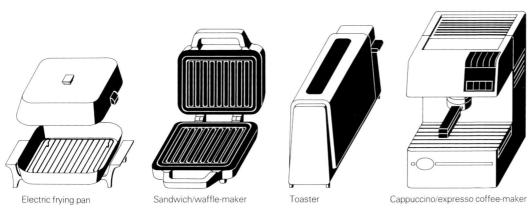

Electric frying pan   Sandwich/waffle-maker   Toaster   Cappuccino/expresso coffee-maker

4

1 *This purpose-built fume extraction hood has been designed as an integral part of a decorative storage system which seems to be suspended from the ceiling. Extraction hoods above island units must be ducted to an outside wall, and require careful planning. Rails fitted to the hood and the worktop keep equipment and utensils within easy reach.*

2 *Here, the stove has been placed against an outside wall, which makes the installation of an extraction hood and ventilation ducting a simpler and less expensive process. The narrow flue links with a wide hood to form a cap above a cooking area which combines electric and gas burners.*

3 *This imaginative solution to the problem of ducting in fume extraction over an island cooking area is in keeping with the overall decorative treatment of this small kitchen. Paintings of the sort usually associated with grand, showpiece rooms appear on the ceiling – an unusual treatment for a small working space. Above, a projectile bird floats in a windswept sky, and below is a pearly marbled floor. In such classical surroundings, it is particularly important not to introduce ungainly appliances. The angled flue of this extraction hood solves the problem of fume extraction from the middle of the room.*

1

2

3

VENTILATION AND EXTRACTION

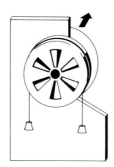
Window ventilator with air pressure rotor

Electric window fan with automatic shutter

Electric wall or window fan with automatic shutter

Recirculating extraction hood with renewable charcoal filter

4

4 *Fume extraction systems are either designed to be as unobtrusive as possible or to look more sculptural than functional, blending inconspicuously with the units and quietly whirring away to remove steam, vapour and cooking smells which quickly become stale. The hi-tech design of this modern kitchen reverses the usual treatment of a utility extraction system, making the technology itself flamboyantly obvious and decorative, both in shape and colour. A gigantic industrial extractor fan, with its silvered, aluminium duct snaking between the shelves, is both purposeful and dominating. The bright blue canopy above the stove further highlights the extraction equipment in the best hi-tech style, where bright primary colours are used to pick out utilitarian fittings against a white background. The window frame is given the same dramatic treatment.*
In hi-tech interiors, industrial materials and fittings are employed. Whenever possible the services which are usually hidden, such as wiring, ducting and pipes, are exposed and highlighted in a celebration of engineering. Everything in this domestic kitchen has been borrowed from its intended factory setting and adapted for home use, including the unusual suspended storage system clamped to the ceiling pipes.

DUCTING FOR FUME EXTRACTION

Cooking produces a great deal of steam, which can lead to harmful condensation. Cooking fumes laden with grease and fat also discolour surfaces, and leave lingering smells. The most efficient solution is to install a fume extractor hood and fan above the stove. If the stove is set against an outside wall, the fan can be directly mounted into the wall; otherwise, measure and saw PVC ducting to carry fumes and steam away from the stove to an outside wall, connecting the pieces together with the appropriate fitting. Ducting should be kept as short as possible. Less expensive solutions than ducted extraction include the type of hood which recirculates grease-laden air through a charcoal filter, or a separate window or wall fan or ventilator (see opposite).

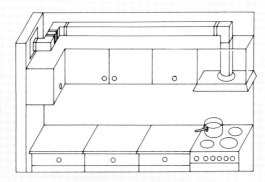

1 *Someone whose cooking interest is limited to ready-prepared foods for the microwave will be able to stash the necessary implements in a handy drawer. But even if it were possible to find a cupboard to accommodate the odd shapes and sizes of the pans, sieves, scales and other gadgets displayed here, the active cook might still prefer to have them close to hand, on a wall rack or on the worktop. This wire display grid, scaled to a larger size than the gridded wallpaper of this formally appointed small kitchen, is practical for the active cook.*

2 *This unusual kitchen storage cupboard is recessed into the wall and fitted with two stainless steel rails from which a range of utensils hangs on hooks. The pull-down stainless steel shutter and its burnished frame are appropriate in this sleek grey and black kitchen, whose owner does not like the cluttered look of equipment on display.*

3 *This island room divider-cum-storage unit would make a fine open display of decorative tableware. Instead, it is packed with more tools of the active cook: storage jars and boxes of food, as well as a library of cookbooks. Extra racks hang from wooden ledges to hold knives, paper towels, plastic wrap and assorted spices and condiments.*

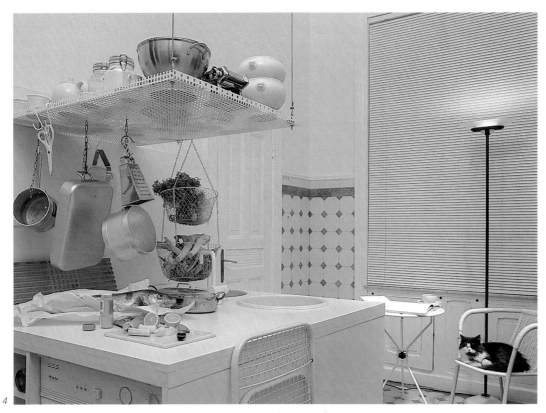

4 *This square peninsular work station with a built-in stove top and sink has a sheet of perforated steel hanging above the hard-to-reach central worktop next to the wall. Tableware and storage jars are stashed on top, while the cook's immediate needs – a roasting pan, saucepans, a grater and even wire mesh lettuce drainers adapted to act as hanging vegetable storage bins – are suspended within easy reach.*

5 *When worktop space is limited, a small butcher-block table such as this one, with its slotted rack for storing choppers and knives without dulling the blades, can be a valuable piece of equipment. The solid beech top is ideal for chopping or cutting, and it will last for years if frequently oiled and occasionally sanded. Butcher-block surfaces should not be used near the sink or exposed to water, which will raise the grain of the wood and may cause warping. If placed near the stove, its surface may be marred by burn marks.*

6 *Handy hanging systems for utensils need not be limited to kitchens with abundant overhead or under-shelf space. Here, beech ledges battened to the wall support the ubiquitous hanging hooks for utensils, special utensil racks and a shelf with storage boxes.*

The sink is perhaps the most basic piece of large kitchen equipment. Even the smallest kitchen, where cooking is a question of heating up a can of soup on a countertop hot plate, will have a sink for washing up. Modern sinks are available in a staggering variety of shapes, sizes, colours and materials – there is something to suit every conceivable kitchen decor. They are now usually made from stainless steel or enamelled steel, and can range from a simple bowl set into a counter to twin sinks separated by a small sink with a waste-disposal unit, complete with a range of custom-fitting accessories such as drainer baskets with plate racks, cutting boards and strainer bowls which extend the work surface of the countertop when the sink is not needed. Traditionalists can still find china sinks to round out an authentic country-style kitchen. Although their surface is more susceptible than others to cracking and chipping, they tend to be larger and may be the only choice when a free-standing sink is necessary.

1 These large, deep, moulded double sinks are an integral part of the countertop. All are made from Corian, a hard-wearing and stain-resistant mineral-filled plastic that feels like marble. As with natural materials such as wood, any surface damage can be easily repaired by sanding.

1

SINKS

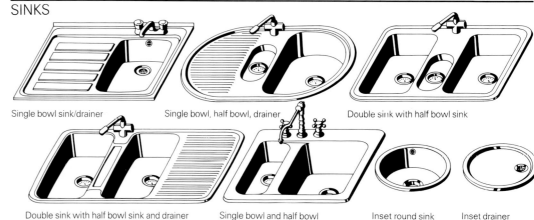

Single bowl sink/drainer   Single bowl, half bowl, drainer   Double sink with half bowl sink

Double sink with half bowl sink and drainer   Single bowl and half bowl   Inset round sink   Inset drainer

2

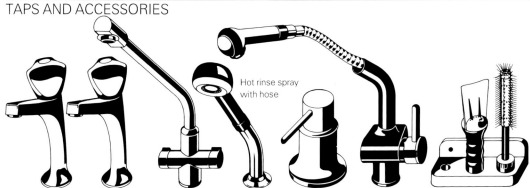

TAPS AND ACCESSORIES

Hot rinse spray
with hose

Pair of traditional stand-up
taps (non-mixing)

Designer mixer tap
with swivelling spout

Liquid soap
dispenser

Mixer tap with built-in extractable
spray and cleaning attachments

2 *Despite the advent of steel sinks enamelled in all colours of the rainbow, many kitchens are fitted with one of the innumerable stainless steel models available. Stainless steel is more hard-wearing than vitreous enamel, although even its surface can become dulled in time from myriad tiny scratches. To retain the original smoothly burnished look, the sink and drainer should be buffed with a cloth after use. Stainless steel sinks are appropriate in almost any decor, from countrified kitchens with wooden cabinets and quarry tiles on the floor to rooms decorated in flowery pastels. The minimal, almost industrial style of this kitchen could easily have been inspired by the eminently practical double stainless steel sink fitted into the matt charcoal countertop. The kitchen is decorated entirely in shades of grey, with unusual perforated aluminium doors which echo the steely grey of the sink.*
Unlike more homely arrangements, with cooking utensils hanging from the walls and appliances lining the countertops, here everything is stored away out of sight. A drainer basket for clean dishes can fit into one of the deep rectangular bowls, eliminating unsightly countertop clutter, and a spray attachment on an extendible hose has been fitted in alongside the swivelling mixer tap.

1 *At first glance, this appears to be a traditional china sink with old brass taps. It is in fact entirely modern, right down to the mixer tap and cross-head faucets, and is made from enamelled steel. The enamel finish is five times thicker than usual, which gives a deep, chip-resistant gloss which looks like an old-style ceramic finish. A closer look at its gently curving lines reveals its modern manufacture.*

2 *Although sinks are most often associated with the tedious chore of washing up after a meal, they are also the focus of much food preparation. Modern sinks have numerous optional accessories to assist the shift from one activity to the other. Here, a single sink with a fitted drainer basket, a small central sink with a fitted vegetable strainer and a counter-level drainer may make better use of space than a double sink. For maximum utility, a waste-disposal unit can be fitted to the small central sink.*

3 *This elegant white-enamelled bowl and drainer sink is designed to be extremely practical. A built-in inset drainer sufficiently recessed to prevent water from seeping on to the surrounding worktop is useful both for drying dishes and for washing vegetables. As with so many modern sink sets, a matching designer mixer tap is an optional extra.*

DISH DRAINERS

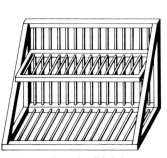
Wall-mounted wooden dish drainer

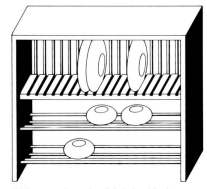
Wall-mounted wooden dish drainer/display

Wire drainer basket to fit sink

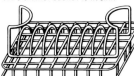
Wire drainer basket for counter

4

5

6

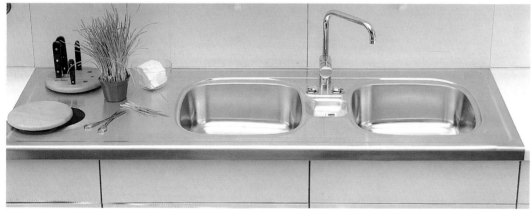

7

WASTE DISPOSAL

Waste disposal units are especially valuable for urban apartment dwellers with limited space to accommodate the rubbish which can build up between weekly collections. They are best installed in kitchens with at least a double sink, or with a sink unit containing a large single sink and a half bowl to the side for the waste disposal unit as shown here, which is particularly effective in association with a dishwasher. Waste disposal units occupy a good deal of under-sink storage space, but will take care of all organic rubbish. If hard waste disposal is also a problem, you should consider a waste compactor, which compresses everything that cannot go into the waste disposal into manageable units.

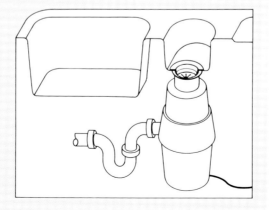

4 *The cupboards below a sink generally disguise its plumbing requirements, which can occupy much of their storage potential. The best use for the remaining space is to house cleaning materials and a rubbish bin. Kitchen manufacturers have developed ingenious systems for making garbage disposal as handy and space-saving as possible.*
This rubbish bin is designed to be mounted on the inside of a cupboard door. When the door is opened, a special mechanism lifts the dustbin lid.

5 *Here, a panel which matches the cupboard doors, hinged at the bottom and fitted with a guard chain, drops open to reveal an attached rubbish bin.*

6 *This pull-out bin is an ideal solution for under-sink rubbish. A deep tray mounted on easy-sliding runners is fronted by a panel which matches the kitchen cupboard doors. The narrow garbage bin attached to the inside of the panel is as large as it can be without interfering with the plumbing.*

7 *The drainer portion of this commodious double sink incorporates a hole for dropping rubbish through into the garbage bin below the counter. The circular, solid beech cover doubles as a small chopping board. Behind, a matching block keeps knives accessible without dulling their blades.*

Storage needs vary enormously from household to household. To discover your needs, a professional kitchen designer would ask the following questions: how many people live in the house or apartment, how many meals do you prepare a day, what sort of food do you like, how much cooking equipment do you use, how many sets of crockery do you own, do you eat in a separate dining room with its own storage facilities? Once they have approximately calculated the amount and type of storage required, it is said, they usually double it.

Obviously, the large family with a double oven, dishwasher, crockery and equipment that has accumulated for years and a tendency to buy basic foodstuffs in bulk, will require substantially more storage space than the single person who grabs one hasty meal a day at home and does not want a life cluttered with unnecessary possessions. You already have a very useful guide to your needs, namely your present storage system and how well it works.

The amount of equipment, gadgetry, glasses, cutlery and china you possess is not difficult to quantify and plan for, but you have to decide whether you want it hidden behind attractive fitted units or on display. Another important consideration is ease of access – remembering to place heavy objects at lower levels and things which are in constant use close at hand. Bending and searching for everyday pots and pans becomes a nuisance, which is why busy cooks often hang them from hooks where they can be easily reached without getting in the way. Whether shelves are open or behind doors, they must be planned so that they are not too deep at higher levels where objects at the back cannot be seen or reached. Safety is another factor since young children will find knives and glassware endlessly fascinating if they are within reach.

The same is true of potentially dangerous cleaning products. Dishcloths, sponges, dustpans, brushes and larger brooms and vacuum cleaners can create chaos if not properly stored.

Canned and dry foods are usually easy to plan for, but fresh food is the ever-changing item in the kitchen – expanding after shopping expeditions and shrinking quickly after a family feast. Versatile ventilated larder units and smaller food storage units with fitted wire baskets for vegetables and compartments for bread are now available. Refrigerators and freezers – either separate or combined – offer a very wide choice in terms of size and function and require as much research as cookers do in order to ensure the right choice.

Whatever the size of your kitchen, whether it is a small galley dedicated to cooking or an all-purpose family room, your storage requirements will compete for space with the working equipment of the room. Fortunately, modern kitchen systems are designed to incorporate every convenience you can imagine – from cooking appliances to laundry facilities – so as to maximize storage space.

There was a day when separate rooms fulfilled many of the storage functions of the modern kitchen: the galley-like butler's pantry between the dining room and kitchen was lined with shelves and drawers for tableware, glasses and linens; a naturally cool walk-in larder was reserved for foodstuffs; a separate laundry room kept the washing, drying and ironing of clothes out of the cook's way. Today, in addition to its traditional food-preparation function, the kitchen often has to be a dining room, pantry, larder, laundry, wine cellar and even play room – all rolled into one. The more efficiently you can store things, the better.

Kitchen storage is all about organization. Equipment, accessories and ingredients should be stored nearest to the place where they are likely to be used. Pans or utensils in frequent use should be within easy reach, somewhere between eye and knee level. Open-shelf storage systems, like the one illustrated here, are suitable for an organized cook with naturally tidy instincts.

1 *The numerous fitted cupboards of this sophisticated kitchen provide more than enough storage space for most purposes. Items stored in full view or behind glazed doors are those whose colour or shape contribute to the overall decor, where subtle natural tones predominate. Perfect pigeon-hole rows of cups and bowls look extremely elegant against the cool natural textures and colours of sand and pure white. Even the wall cupboards, which are glazed with wire glass, display tableware which contributes to the overall theme. Major appliances which do not fit in with the scheme are fitted with decor panels that match the cupboard doors. The white façade of the built-in oven, a fan-assisted model which cooks faster at lower temperatures, is featured as part of a white theme that embraces some cupboard doors, tableware, storage jars, saucepans, the countertop and even the taps. The unusual panes of the Japanese-style window throw soft pools of light on to the work area near the sink.*

1

2

3

2 *When is a kitchen not a kitchen? An un-kitchen appearance is especially important where kitchens double as living rooms. It is possible to house kitchen requisites without installing storage units specially designed for the kitchen. In this tiny living area, the tile-covered open storage shelves serve admirably.*

3 *Designers of modern kitchens have developed something of a fetish about dish drainers, which they would prefer to see banished for ever from sight. The practical reality for most of us is that dishes dry more hygienically and with much less work on their own, in purpose-made drainers exposed to air circulation. In this tiny kitchen with limited space for wall cupboards, the problems of draining washed dishes and of storing them once dried are both solved with a single space-saving and decorative open-shelf system. It is unusual to find the sink sited any place other than on an outside wall, where the water supply is usually located. Because this sink is fitted into the peninsular worktop-cum-breakfast counter, the three-tier dish draining rack suspended from the ceiling helps to visually screen the kitchen area from the living area while retaining a light, open atmosphere.*

Cunning fittings inside cupboard doors make each kitchen individual, even when it is made up of standard units. Explore the most basic kitchen and you will discover that the act of opening the door also opens the lid of a rubbish bin fitted inside. There are countless possibilities.

1 *Corner space is often wasted, since the contents of deep corner cupboards are generally inaccessible. These half-round plastic-coated wire carousels make it easy to find whatever saucepan or implement is required without rummaging in the dark depths of the corner cupboard. The lower carousel swings out to reveal its contents when the door is opened.*

2 *This corner unit is designed to make the most of wasted corner space. A double-hinged door permits three-quarter-round carousels to spin around and out, so that any item stored inside is within easy reach in seconds.*

3 *An imitation door pulls out to reveal a heavy-duty trolley which fits below the counter when not in use. A protective rail and attached basket keep contents firmly in place.*

4 *These pull-out shelves store all the appliances and attachments you could ever want to use with the food processing unit built into the worktop above.*

1

2

3

4

5

6

7

8

5 *This tall larder unit makes good use of a narrow corner for storing food supplies. At its lowest level, a round carousel shelf provides easy access to dry goods, with reserve items stashed on shelves above. A sliding roll-down door conceals this clever treatment of a difficult space.*

6 *Often it is more sensible to keep china behind closed doors, rather than displaying it on the shelves of a dresser, which takes up more space than stacking. China can be astonishingly heavy, and needs to be stored on secure shelves. The sturdy adjustable shelving fitted in this wall cupboard wastes no space. Stacks of plates and soup bowls require shallower shelving than cups and jugs: shelves can be adjusted to accommodate the maximum amount of china. The hinges, developed especially for laid-on kitchen cabinet doors, prevent doors from snapping and swinging shut abruptly.*

7 *The space below a built-in cooker top is ideal for storing saucepans and baking tins. Even the plinth at the floor can house shallow cake pans.*

8 *To save bending over and searching through lower cupboards for a saucepan stored at the back, consider instead these pull-out shelves on easy-sliding runners.*

Refrigerators and freezers are now available in shapes, sizes and colours to suit every requirement. Some are free-standing, and others are designed to be housed in built-in units and concealed by decor panels which match the kitchen cupboard doors. Some can sit on top of the counter, and others fit underneath it, pulling out on smooth slides like deep drawers. It is possible to find everything from a simple refrigerator with a small freezer compartment, to stacking refrigerator and freezer units, to side-by-side combination refrigerator/freezers, to large independent freezer chests. Only you will know which of the many fittings available are essential to your requirements.

1　*The owner of this comfortable family kitchen has painted the built-in units a warm, glossy cream colour which looks good with the bleached boards of the old stripped pine table. Incorporating large white appliances such as this combination refrigerator/freezer into an integrated kitchen decor poses a difficult challenge. However, its ample capacity is ideal for someone with limited shopping time who must nonetheless get a meal on the table every day. The ice cube dispenser built into the freezer door adds a touch of luxury, and is useful for entertaining.*

1

STORAGE TIMES FOR FRESH FOODS

	Refrigerated	Frozen		Refrigerated	Frozen
Bacon, packed for deep freeze	–	5 months	Butter, salted	3-4 weeks	3 months
Bacon rashers, green	7 days	1 month	Casseroles with bacon	2 days	3 months
Bacon rashers, smoked	7 days	1½ months	Casseroles without bacon	3 days	6 months
Bacon rashers, vacuum-packed	7 days	3 months	Cheese, hard	7 days	6 months
Beef, large roasts and joints	3-5 days	12 months	Cheese, soft	4-5 days	3 months
Beef, steaks and small cuts	3-5 days	8 months	Chicken	1-3 days	12 months
Beef, minced	3-5 days	3 months	Duck	1-3 days	4-6 months
Bread	3-6 days	2-6 months	Eggs	3 weeks	1 month
Bread dough	–	3 months	Fish, cooked	1 day	2 months
Butter and fats	2-3 weeks	6 months	Fish, raw	1-2 days	4-6 months

2

3

	Refrigerated	Frozen
Fish, smoked	3-4 days	3 months
Fruit, soft (without sugar)	1-5 days	6 months
Ham	2-3 days	2 months
Lamb, large joints	3-5 days	8 months
Lamb, chops and noisettes	3-5 days	6 months
Lamb, cubed for stews	3-5 days	4 months
Leftovers	1 day	–
Milk and cream	3-5 days	–
Offal	1-2 days	2-3 months
Pastry, uncooked	2 days	3-6 months

	Refrigerated	Frozen
Pork, large roasts or cuts	2-4 days	6 months
Pork, chops	2-4 days	4 months
Sausages	3 days	3 months
Shellfish, fresh	1 day	2 months
Shellfish, defrosted	use at once	never refreeze
Soups, stocks and sauces	3-6 days	2-3 months
Turkey	2 days	4-6 months
Veal, large roasts or joints	2-4 days	6 months
Veal, chops or cutlets	2-4 days	3 months
Vegetables, green	1-5 days	12 months

2 *This small refrigerator, designed to be built in under the countertop, manages to incorporate a great deal of storage capacity and would be good for a kitchen with limited space. It has a small freezer compartment at the top, plastic-coated wire shelves with hinged flaps to accommodate large bottles and two lower bins for vegetables or other odd-shaped foods. Door fittings include a compartment for butter and cheese, a lipped shelf with an egg rack and a bottle rack with retaining rail.*

3 *This three-part built-in refrigerator illustrates the immense versatility of modern food storage systems. The upper portion incorporates a large freezing compartment. Although it would probably be insufficient for a green-fingered vegetable gardener with vast quantities of fresh produce to preserve, it would certainly do for a busy cook who wants to keep a moderate stock of frozen food on hand. The shelves of the main food storage area are adjustable, which minimizes wasted space above shallow items and makes it possible to accommodate unusually tall bottles when necessary. The lower portion is a pull-out, 'cellar-cool' storage cabinet, ideal for chilling fresh fruit, vegetables and beverages.*

Before the advent of refrigeration, foodstuffs were stored in the larder, a cool, ventilated room or cupboard located on an east- or north-facing wall. For many, a cool larder is still the preferred place to store many foods whose flavour is diminished by excessive chilling. In modern homes with no ventilated larder, a 'cellar-cool' storage cabinet like the one illustrated on page 37 is another option. Although the refrigerator has replaced the larder for cold foodstuff storage to a great extent, most modern kitchens will still require a special storage facility for those foodstuffs which do not require refrigeration.

1 Fruit and vegetables can be stored in well-ventilated, deep, plastic-coated wire baskets on easy-glide runners in a cool, dark cupboard.

2 These shallow plastic-coated wire racks, which slide forward to make items stored in the back easily accessible, are ideal for hard-to-store goods.

3 This pull-out storage rack is intended for tall objects, such as bottles and French bread.

4 Dried goods such as salt, spices, flour and sugar can benefit from storage in wooden boxes. These pigeon-hole stacking drawers provide easy access to perishables.

1

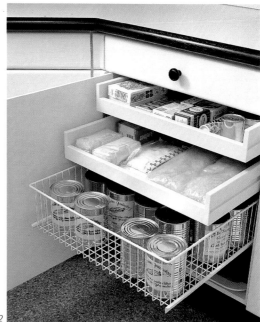
2

3

4

5

5 *The storage fittings developed by the manufacturers of standard kitchen units make best use of every inch of precious space, but are of little interest when it is not feasible completely to rebuild a kitchen, since they are generally designed to fit inside the manufacturer's own units. When it is not possible to adopt purpose-built food storage systems, there are many imaginative options. Dry foodstuffs can be decanted into decorative storage jars and displayed on an open shelf, rather than being stashed away, still in their original plastic bags, in a tray like the one illustrated opposite (2).*
This modern wood dresser bridges the gap between the modern kitchen, where every element is built in, and the older kitchen, with its motley assortment of free-standing furniture and appliances. Instead of the usual rank of treasured plates, the glazed upper cabinet displays a colourful assortment of home preserves and storage jars containing dried foodstuffs. It is all too easy for the work of preserving fresh fruits and vegetables at their prime to be forgotten months later when the jars are stuffed away in an inaccessible cupboard. This unusual solution contributes to a homespun atmosphere, with its combination of traditional-style furniture, natural wood and array of foodstuffs.

1 *A room dedicated to laundry – from washing and drying to ironing – is a luxury few modern homeowners could contemplate. But sooner or later most people will add at least a washing machine to their list of essential appliances. The kitchen, with its water inlet and outlet plumbing, is the most logical location for home laundry facilities. Front-loading washing machines fit below the worktop or extend its surface. Combination washer-dryers which do not require outside ducting are ideal for a small apartment kitchen. For larger rooms, consider stacking washing machines and dryers, or commodious free-standing appliances.*

In this spacious utility area, a stacking washing machine and separate dryer have been installed in special units manufactured for the purpose next to a large sink near an outside wall. Full advantage has been taken of the range of special units available to provide a superbly equipped laundry/utility area for a big family.

The roller ironing machine, operated by a treadle from a comfortable chair, makes ironing sheets and tablecloths a relatively painless process, even in a busy big household. It folds up and rolls into a tall storage cupboard which also houses mops, brooms and other tall objects – including a conventional ironing board.

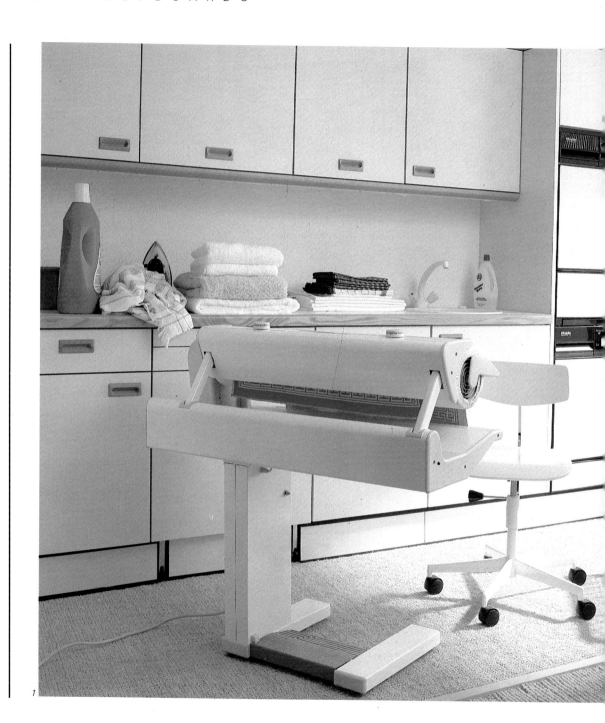

1

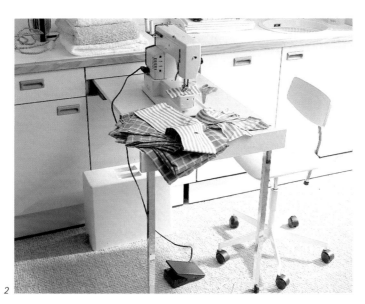

2 *When planning laundry and other utility storage, modern kitchen manufacturers have not forgotten the number of odd-shaped and bulky items to be accommodated in connection with washing and cleaning, from laundry and ironing gear to everyday cleaning fluids, mops and brooms. Special storage cupboard fittings allow for the awkward shapes and sizes. This close-up view of the utility area shown opposite reveals a stable hideaway work table. Here, it is used as a sewing table when the portable sewing machine stored in the cupboard below is needed.*

3 *The unit next to the sink in the utility area shown opposite opens to reveal a cupboard front panel with an attached trolley. A feature of many manufactured kitchens, this one is fitted near the laundry machines, with a plastic-coated wire bin to act as a handy laundry basket.*

4 *Plumbing beneath the sink can be a hindrance to storage. This plastic-coated wire storage rack attaches to the back of the cupboard door, and maximizes use of an often cluttered area.*

5 *All-purpose, tall utility cupboards provide an intelligent solution to most ordinary utility storage. The combination of hooks and shelves keeps cleaning tools and appliances ready for use.*

Kitchen surfaces take more battering and scrubbing than any other surfaces in the house. If kitchen surfaces mark easily this creates more work because of extra cleaning and more expense because they will not last. Surfaces also play a large part in determining the style and visual impact of the kitchen, so when choosing them it is vital to think in terms of durability and not be entirely seduced by appearance. Good looks are important, but so are strength and quality. Fortunately, modern kitchen surfaces are made from such a wide range of natural and man-made materials that it is always possible to find something which will suit the style of your kitchen decor, your working requirements and your budget.

Surfaces for cupboard doors are directly related to the cost of units. The cheapest are doors made from chipboard with a paper-thin laminate finish. In the middle range are solid laminates and wood veneers; and then combinations of laminate with wood trims and solid wood. Shapely doors with moulded panels or specialist finishes such as staining, lacquering and hand painting, including effects like dragging or marbling, all make the price go up significantly. Fashion influences finishes – golden pine is popular one year and grey laminate the next – and technology does too. The latest immensely durable and resistant surface being used by German kitchen manufacturers uses car-factory techniques of dipping whole units in polystyrene colour which is surface sealed and then baked to a really hard, tough consistency.

Worktops need to be even more wear resistant to take sharp knives and hot pans as well as messy stains and constant scrubbing. Few modern alternatives can compete with the traditional worktops of solid marble or hardwood, such as beech, which clean easily and age graciously. They are also among the most expensive options. Tiles are attractive but the grouting between them usually stains – always use heavy-duty non-porous grout and high-quality tiles. Marble-like materials, such as Corian, can be hard-wearing. Laminates are not usually so successful unless chopping is always done on a board and hot pans are placed on mats. Laminates vary and the most expensive are usually the most hard-wearing. Other alternatives include luxury burnished steel, granite or slate.

Having assessed the quality and durability of a surface you then have to choose the colour, pattern, wood grain and any decorative details or other options. Remember that you will have to live with your choice for some time so try not to be too heavily influenced by sales talk or fashion considerations. Bright red may look stunning in a well-lit open area where it is on display but would be overwhelming in a small city kitchen galley. Even the most spacious and well-planned kitchens are busy, cluttered places, so a neutral background is usually an advantage.

Kitchen surfaces need to withstand a lot of hard treatment and still look good. For this reason, durable laminate countertops and other surfaces have come to feature in many kitchens.

Unlike older laminates, with their thin veneer of coloured plastic laminate, newer products consist of several layers compressed under immense pressure to produce a thicker surface with solid colour throughout. Layers of different colours can be compressed together so that the cut edge of a single-colour surface reveals the different coloured layers like a geological drawing.

Here, a variety of solid-colour core laminates are used: solid white, solid white sandwiched between wood veneer and solid navy similarly sandwiched. The exposed edges of most materials used in kitchen surfaces – the end-grain of wood or the edges of laminate-veneered composite boards – must be protected from moisture, if not concealed.

1   *Worktops vary to suit each cook's particular speciality – and budget. Serious pastry and pasta chefs prefer to work on a white marble top; anyone whose food preparation involves frequent chopping of vegetables for salads, soups and casseroles will use a wooden surface. Slabs or boards made from any material which is especially desirable can always be added.*
The worktop surface which unites your entire kitchen lay-out should be as practical and hard-wearing as possible. Marble, for example, is extremely handsome and prized by pastry cooks, but is neither stain-resistant nor chip-proof. This warm, wooden, country-style kitchen has been entirely fitted with heavy butcher-block worktops made from maple, a handsome hardwood used for the cabinets as well. One drawback to wooden worktops is that standing water can tend to warp the wood or raise its grain. Here, a double stainless steel sink with an ample integral draining board has been fitted to minimize water damage. With use, the smooth surface of this new wooden worktop will become chipped and scratched, but it is best not to consider refinishing it, for evidence of wear will be in keeping with the warm patina which should develop as it ages.

1

HOW TO TILE A WORKTOP

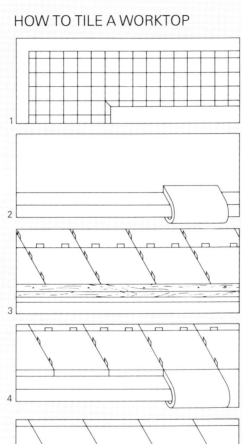

1 Plan worktop tiling so that the cut tile will be next to the wall. **2** Use an edge tile placed in position to mark a base line. **3** Nail a batten to the base line. Spread adhesive and lay the first row of tiles working back from the batten towards the wall, using spacer cards to ensure even spacing between individual tiles. **4** When all the tiles have been laid, remove the batten and spread adhesive on the worktop and on the undersides of the edge tiles. **5** Remove spacer cards. Grout the spaces between the tiles, compacting the grout to finish level with the top of the tiles.

2 *Portable boards for particular jobs – wooden chopping boards, marble pastry boards, stainless steel or plastic draining boards – are indispensable, especially to save wear and tear on all-purpose laminate worktops. Appliances which do the chopping, grinding, blending, slicing or grating save on labour as well as preserving worktops. Unfortunately, electric appliances can easily become wasters of counter space. This well-designed work station solves the problem by housing appliances and their attachments in a shallow cupboard fitted with a handy electric socket where they are easy to reach. With the addition of a wooden chopping block, it becomes a very versatile food preparation area.*

3 *Ceramic tile work surfaces are a favourite in country-style kitchens, although they are not ideal for chopping and their surfaces tend to be uneven. Nonetheless, they are solid, durable and easy to clean so long as they have been installed with impenetrable, water-resistant grout. Here, warm wood and terracotta tiles are juxtaposed over large surface areas – floors, worktops and ceiling – to unify an irregularly shaped kitchen. Large ceramic tiles form an attractive pattern when cut diagonally to fit the sharply angled shape of the worktop.*

1 *The wall area in any kitchen above the worktop and below the wall-mounted cupboards – known as the splashback area – needs to be protected from greasy stains, liquids and other spatters from vigorous mixing, stove-top cooking and dish-washing. The splashback area can be covered with any surface finish that is durable and easy to wipe clean. Even painted plaster with several coats of protective varnish withstands a lot of scrubbing – yacht varnish provides the heaviest-duty protection, as it is designed to hold up against corrosive sprays of salt water. Although it occupies only a small area of wall, the splashback area visually defines the kitchen's work space, providing a link between the lower cupboards with the worktop and the upper cupboards, and it is often given a colourful or patterned treatment. If you inherit a tiled splashback you do not fancy, think twice before you remove the offending tiles, as this will probably lead to replastering the wall. Rather, sacrifice a few millimetres of space and tile over the existing ones using a special adhesive.*
This unusual splashback surface is made from industrial aluminium sheeting with a raised pattern. Its burnished metallic surface softly reflects the lights mounted behind pelmets on the underside of an extended window sill.

1

2

3

HOW TO TILE A WINDOW SILL

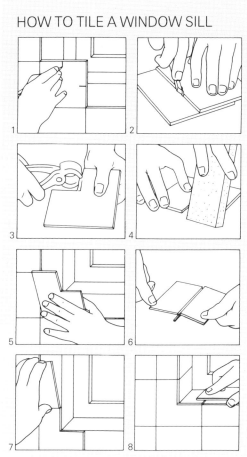

1 To measure a tile for cutting, hold it up to the wall and mark the area to be cut away. **2** Score the glazed surface of the tile along the marked line. **3** For an L-shaped tile, use pincers or tile cutters to remove unwanted waste in small pieces. **4** Use a carborundum stone to clean and smooth the cut edges of the tile. **5** Fix the cut tile so that any spacer lugs are against those of the adjoining tiles. If the tiles you have chosen do not have spacer lugs, use spacer cards to ensure an even gap between tiles. **6** To prepare a tile for breaking, follow steps 1 and 2 above, then place a matchstick under the tile along the scored line for a clean break. **7** Clean the cut edges as in step 4, and fix the cut tile in place. **8** At external corners, make allowance for the tile edge to be covered.

2 *Ordinary wallpaper, which is not washable, only makes a suitable covering for wall surfaces in kitchens equipped with efficient fume extraction systems, and even then it is unsuitable for splashback areas around the sink and stove. Durable, vinyl-coated wallpapers, on the other hand, can be easily wiped clean, although they are more expensive. Here, a dark brown vinyl-coated wallpaper with a white grid pattern echoes the grid pattern on the kitchen cupboard doors and makes a dramatic backdrop for the striking, sculptural extraction hood above the cooker top.*

3 *Ceramic tiles, a traditional favourite for kitchen wall surfaces, present the most hard-wearing, stain-resistant and waterproof option, and are ideal for splashback areas, especially around sinks and stoves. Here, a broad splashback area is covered in ceramic tiles with a small navy and white chequerboard pattern which visually defines the work area against the deep navy cupboards, white worktop and white stove. When unpatterned tiles are used on every available surface, a kitchen can seem cold and clinical. Here, the homy chequered pattern of the tiles in the limited splashback area introduces a warm, enlivening touch in an otherwise sophisticated room.*

1 *Natural wood brings a
welcoming, reassuring sense
of solidity and familiarity to a
kitchen. Unfortunately, the cost
of a custom kitchen built
entirely of solid wood, such as
the one illustrated on page 44,
can be prohibitive. Affordable
wooden kitchens are produced
by using a mixture of solid
wood and wood veneered
board for the visible façade,
with the inside cabinet
carcasses made from less
expensive composite board
with a washable melamine
surface. These economies
make it possible for
manufacturers to offer a wide
range of woods, finishes and
styles. Each timber has its own
characteristic wood grain
pattern, texture and colour, and
these qualities can be
enhanced by the finish applied.
New pine has a bright, clear
yellow colour, and for rustic-
style kitchens boards with
prominent knots are often
used. In its natural state, ash
has a lovely silvery colour,
although it is sometimes more
prized for the beautiful pattern
of its distinctive grain, which is
subtly highlighted when ash is
stained black or a clear bright
colour. Traditional hardwoods,
such as oak, maple or cherry,
may be given a transparent
protective finish to seal the
wood so that the natural colour
shows through, or may be
stained before sealing.*

1

2

3

2 When it is not feasible to install new wooden cabinets, the warmth of natural wood can still contribute to a cosy, friendly atmosphere. This small, family-style kitchen features a hardwood butcher-block worktop which complements the style of the painted cabinets, with their traditional glazed wall cupboards. Butcher-block tabletops and work surfaces are generally made from close-grained hardwoods, such as beech or maple, which are considerably more expensive than softwoods suitable for painting. The addition of wooden furniture reinforces the theme. The owners have also made the most of original timber floorboards by stripping them down to reveal the mellow tones of older wood and applying a durable clear finish.

3 Those who favour laminated plastic surfaces, for whatever reason, can still introduce wood to the kitchen by mixing the two materials. Some manufacturers produce cabinet doors whose frames are made from solid wood, but with laminate-faced board instead of wood-veneered board as the panel. Here, the wooden edges of cool blue laminate worktops and shelves work well with a timber-panelled ceiling. Where uneven walls require replastering, tongue-and-groove timber panelling can cover a multitude of sins.

1 *The great advantage of wood over plastic laminates as a material for cabinet construction is that it can be shaped and moulded into an infinite variety of forms. If this gracious floor-to-ceiling kitchen had been built primarily from laminates, it would have presented a flat facade. Instead, doors and drawer fronts have raised, coffered panels and are set in frames with richly moulded edges. Open display racks are screened by miniature balustrades made from turned wood. By staining the oak cabinets white, the distinctive wood grain remains visible, but a traditional timber kitchen is turned into a light and airy one.*

2 *There has been a revival of interest in specialist paint finishes, which use colour mixtures and texture variations, rather than great blocks of flat colour, to enliven surfaces. Paint or glaze can be added over a background colour with a sponge or by spattering, or a second coat of paint glaze can be partially removed with crumpled rags (called rag-rolling) or special combs (called dragging). The result is a subtly broken colour surface with highly individual effect (depending on the colours and technique used), which gives a charming and distinctive finish to manufactured wooden kitchen cabinets, as in this heavenly blue kitchen.*

1

2

3

3 *The combination of pale blue and white with natural wood is a favourite for kitchens, where it works particularly well. Here, this familiar, informal colour scheme is given a more sophisticated tone by the use of black as an accent. The design takes full advantage of wood as a main material, with slatted door fronts, decorative miniature balustrades on the display shelving and built-in pigeon-hole storage boxes. Cupboards have been custom-built to bend around the difficult corner area. Aside from the natural wood worktop and the main framing of the kitchen – which is white – everything has been painted a refreshing pale blue, from the hinged flap of the extraction hood, to the small spice and salt cellars fixed to the white tiled splashback, to the blue decor panel covering the dishwasher. The warm natural fibres of the sisal carpet echo the wood tones of the worktop, and areas of black are skilfully picked out for emphasis: black stove, black cooking pots and black lacquered bentwood chairs. The pleasing combination of black and white with areas of cool blue demonstrates the importance of distributing colours and accent colours around a room. When painting a new kitchen, or refurbishing an older one, it is best to choose a paint which will withstand washing and wiping.*

1 *Hard-wearing, easy-to-clean plastic laminates are made by bonding layers of resin-impregnated paper together and coating them with plastic. Sheets of plastic laminate are then bonded to chipboard, blockboard or plywood for use in kitchen construction. Improvements in laminate technology have made this practical, relatively inexpensive material even more flexible. A variety of printed, patterned and textured surfaces is available, in addition to a wide range of colours. The edges of plastic laminate worktops can be post-formed so that they are curved, eliminating sharp counter edges. Here, crisp and functional kitchen units made from matt white plastic laminate provide the main structure of a small, friendly kitchen. A treasured rag rug and a collection of bright enamelware displayed on the shelf above the countertop introduce a cheerful, primary colour scheme. Great care has been taken to ensure that all accessories contribute to the theme of red accents, from the trim on the kitchen units, to the Venetian blinds, taps, sink, draining board, hob and shelf uprights and brackets – right down to the floor cupboard plinths. A wooden pine floor and stripped pine door create a warm golden background and enhance the countrified air of this room.*

1

2

3

2 *A chic effect is achieved here by combining pale grey with white trim and appliances and bright yellow accessories. A somewhat different effect could be achieved simply by using red or blue accessories. With subtle shades like grey and white it is important to create some visual contrasts for interest. Here a tablecloth with a bold black and white pattern has been introduced.*

3 *Although plastic laminate surfaces are often chosen because they provide good value for money, they can also play an important role in achieving an elegant interior. Here, intelligent design and planning have teamed ordinary white plastic laminates with more exotic materials – wood and chrome – to create a kitchen which is both stylish and practical. A large wooden peninsular counter extends from the white façade next to the stove, doubling as worktop and table for impromptu dining. Chrome drawer and door handles are echoed by a chrome draining board with built-in circular knife storage block and refuse disposal chute. Special storage compartments house bread, herbs, spices and even a foldaway stepladder in a plinth panel drawer.*

Refitting a kitchen from scratch is an expensive business. Sometimes a change of colour and attention to detail can create all the difference to standard kitchen units. Colourful lipped handles, 'D'-handles and knobs with coloured laminate trims can be added to doors, drawers and panels to brighten up dull units. A more profound change can still be achieved by replacing only the doors and drawer fronts of an existing kitchen. Some manufacturers supply doors in a range of colours which fit standard kitchen units. Or create an eye-catching new look at minimal expense by staining or painting old kitchen units. A bright finish in a new colour can transform a kitchen. Surfaces can be textured with a specialist paint finish, such as rag-rolling or sponging, or decorative patterns can be painted on using a stencil cut for the purpose.

1 The moulded edges of the frames of these doors and drawer fronts have been deepened and highlighted by a finely painted line. Ceramic knobs and pulls look good with the dragged paint finish.

2 Here, a more baroque treatment of door frames has elaborately moulded edges on both frame and raised coffered panels.

6

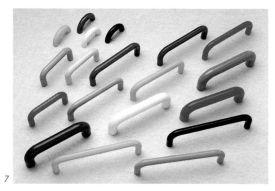

7

8

SPECIALIST PAINT FINISHES

 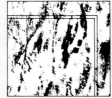

Rag-rolling creates an attractive two-tone 'distressed' paint finish. Roll a wadded cloth over a wet glaze which you have brushed on top of a dried first coat of paint.

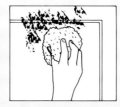 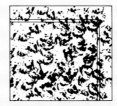

Sponging produces a two-tone variegated surface. Dip a natural sponge into a pan of wet glaze and then sponge the glaze over a dried first coat of paint.

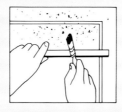 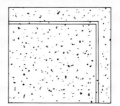

Spattering produces multicolour patterning. Fleck droplets of glaze on to a dried first coat of paint by passing a metal ruler over the glaze-filled bristles of a paintbrush.

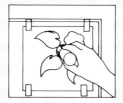 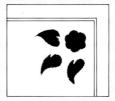

Stencilling adds figurative interest. Make a stencil from waterproof paper and use quick-drying paint and a stencil brush to paint the pattern on to a prepared surface.

3 Natural wood lends itself well to the design of these doors and drawer fronts. The deep frames and raised inner panels have a curved shape which is highlighted by their elaborately moulded edges.

4 The D-shaped plastic handles on this simple white laminate drawer front and door continue as a dramatic line stretched across the surface, which adds not only a splash of colour but also dynamic interest.

5 The edges of these white plastic laminate doors and drawer fronts have been angled and finished with chrome to provide very stylish detailing, which is reinforced by the handsome chrome handles. The angled edges of raised panels or frames are often outlined or picked out by a contrast in colour. Here, an unusual effect is achieved by a similar use of contrast in material.

6 Plastic handles, pulls and knobs, such as the small selection illustrated here, can be chosen to co-ordinate with a range of other accessories to brighten a room.

7 Some manufacturers let buyers of their kitchen units choose which colour they prefer from a range of 'D'-handles.

8 Plastic door and drawer furniture can take any shape.

The kitchen floor needs to be the toughest in the house because of wear from the constant movement of feet and chair legs and also because of spillage, scuffing, heat and the occasional heavy knock from a falling frying pan or bottle. It must be easy to clean, non-slip for safety and water-resistant. It is not an aspect of the kitchen that can be chosen on looks alone, but looks are important and the floor you select must complement the style of the room. Always seek professional advice about laying floors if you are not experienced, since a potentially excellent floor can be ruined if it is badly laid, the wrong adhesive is used or the sub-floor not adequately prepared. It is often necessary to put down a flat layer of board to even out irregular concrete or floorboards which can create dents and may not be a suitable base for the flooring you have selected.

The least expensive and most flexible choice is usually sheet vinyl, which can be applied to most floor surfaces and is available in a wide variety of qualities and strengths, with cushion backing, and every kind of colour and pattern from fake marble to stylish modern grid and chequered designs. Vinyl tiles are similarly varied and easily extended or replaced provided you buy in excess rather than try to match existing tiles at a later date.

Treated cork is warm, resilient and does not show the dirt. Like vinyl, it has the advantage of causing fewer breakages if china or glassware is dropped and it is a quiet surface. Terrazzo, a surface composed of marble chips, quarry tiles or marble slips set in concrete, is rather cold and hard, but extremely hard-wearing and attractive. The same is true of ceramic tiles, which also have the advantage of creating colourful or unusual designs, depending on the pattern in which they are laid.

Linoleum, available in sheets or tiles, has been much improved by new technology and is no longer the brittle substance it once was. It is now available with a durable, non-scuff plastic finish and in designs of great sophistication. It is not cheap and some of the most attractive designs are among the most expensive options for your kitchen floor. Other luxury surfaces include slate and traditional flagstone, but they must be laid on a solid floor that can withstand the weight of these materials.

Polished wood is warm and long-lasting but needs regular polishing and frequent resealing in areas of heavy wear. Painted wood and carpet are not advisable for kitchens. There are several ways to achieve a polished wood floor, depending on your kitchen decor and budget. For a country-style kitchen in an older home, simply refinish existing floorboards by stripping off existing tiles or sheet flooring, sanding the floorboards back to clean wood and applying a hard-wearing sealer. Otherwise, lay new hardwood floorboards or wood strip tiles which emulate elaborate parquet flooring.

A black and white chequerboard floor is in bold contrast to the clean lines and quiet restraint of this large kitchen, but perfectly in keeping with its styling, which is that of a turn-of-the-century dairy. The kitchen units, with their homy tongue-and-groove timber panel doors, have been painted with a glossy cream-coloured paint. A wooden worktop below a long row of many-paned windows follows the A-line of the roof. Despite its old-style atmosphere, full advantage has been taken of available space to install large modern appliances. Large chequerboard patterned floors can also work well in smaller rooms. Vinyl or linoleum tiles can be laid in alternating colours. Sheet vinyl or linoleum with chequerboard patterning is also available.

1   *A pattern of small white diamond insets against a rich navy blue makes a bold flooring to anchor a relatively casual alignment of pine kitchen units with sliding doors and open shelves in three widths set above. This treatment draws the eye to the kitchen and provides a dramatic backdrop for a simple pine kitchen table. The fresh colour combination is echoed in reverse by the fine blue floral motif on the white tiles of the splashback.*

2   *Polished wooden floorboards make both a good foil for a fine tapestry rug in the living room and a handsome, practical kitchen floor in this comfortable open-plan house. The eye is drawn from the wooden farmhouse table and ladderback chairs to the deep, glossy green of the kitchen units. The rocking chair and dresser are in keeping with this theme of natural forest colours and woods.*

1

2

3

3 *This subdued grey floor, made up of synthetic rubber floor tiles, is eminently practical and provides an ideal backdrop for the fresh look of this white plastic laminate self-assembly kitchen. The tiles echo the colour of the stainless steel sink and drainer and the grey-painted slatted blinds. Deep green 'D'-handles are matched by green accessories and objects: a Perrier bottle, apples, bottle lids, laundry basket, bucket and dish draining rack. A simple unplastered brick column which reinforces the wall in this open-plan kitchen also screens the laundry area, providing a niche large enough to house appliances and utility cupboards.*

Although this relatively large kitchen area incorporates a convenient laundry centre and plenty of storage space, its design takes advantage of relatively inexpensive components.

Simple, self-assembly kitchen units can cost considerably less than a kitchen installed by specialists. Synthetic rubber floor tiles represent good value for money, especially when covering a large floor area such as this one.

1   *Glazed ceramic floor tiles, which are sold in packs with laying instructions, can be a great deal more stylish when they are laid with a border pattern. Here, black tiles interspersed with the primary white floor tiles to form a pattern give definition to the outer edge of a large room. Tiles can also be laid diagonally, point to point, or smaller tiles can form a houndstooth pattern. Frostproof ceramic tiles can form a continuous floor surface for a kitchen with a door opening on to a patio garden.*

2   *Vinyl sheet flooring is immensely practical and easy to install. The simple diagonal line pattern of this vinyl sheet flooring visually extends the eye, making a room seem slightly larger. This material is ideal for both kitchen and laundry room floors, since it is easily cleaned with a mop and water. Its smooth, cushioned surface is warm and comfortable for bare feet. Vinyl sheet flooring can be laid loose with double-sided tape at doorways and seams, or it can be firmly stuck in place with tiling adhesive.*

1

2

HOW TO LAY CORK OR VINYL FLOOR TILES

Mark the centre of the room by stretching a chalked line taut between pins tacked into the floor or skirting in the middle of facing walls about 25mm (1in) above the floor. Snap the chalked line to leave a chalk mark on the floor. On long lengths, press the centre of the chalked string on the floor and snap each side in turn. If you wish, substitute any light powder for chalk.

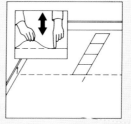

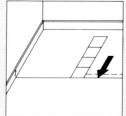

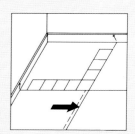

1 Mark the centre of the chalk line and lay a 'dry' row of tiles out to an end wall.

2 If the end gap is 75mm (3in) or less, snap a new line half a tile width from the first.

3 Repeat the procedure with a chalked line and row of tiles at right angles to the first.

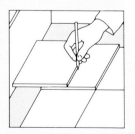

4 Spread adhesive over the lines and snap fresh lines when it is dry.

5 Lay the first tiles in the corner of the lines, then lay tiles to form a pyramid shape.

6 Lower each tile into place, butting it tightly against the adjacent tiles.

7 Score edge tiles with a knife and then bend sharply to complete the break.

3 *Warm cork tiles add natural colour to any room and are appropriate in a kitchen so long as they are well sealed. They are available in different shades. Pre-sanded cork tiles must be sealed with polyurethane varnish – preferably several coats – after they are laid. Some can be bought already sealed with polyurethane varnish, and some have a vinyl skin surface which is extremely durable. The fine diagonal lines on these sealed cork tiles transform this everyday flooring into a bold definition of space. They can be used to create a pattern in one area, say in the centre of a room where furniture is grouped, with plain cork tiles occupying the rest of the floor area.*

4 *Terracotta-coloured floor tiles and quarry tiles are traditionally a favourite for country-style and farmhouse kitchens.*

5 *Synthetic rubber floor tiles, with their characteristic raised circular pattern, first appeared in hi-tech kitchens and interiors, borrowed from the industrial settings where they were first used. Even the lighter-duty tiles now made for domestic use, which are available in a vast range of colours, have superb wearing properties: they are easy to lay, comfortable to walk on and easy to look after. Try laying tiles of two or more colours for a patterned effect.*

1 *Task lighting is a rather intimidating phrase which simply means what it says: lighting which illuminates the task in hand. In the kitchen, this particularly refers to the worktop area. The advantage of wall-mounted cupboards is that they present a surface area at precisely the right height above the worktop for a light to be fitted, shielded by a narrow pelmet. Manufacturers often build lighting strips into the base of the wall-hung cupboards, but you can also fit them yourself to an existing kitchen. Fluorescent light is the favoured source, since it lasts longest for the least money. This is the light of the supermarkets, a rather cold light above food – which is why the new tungsten halogen sources are finding favour. Solid wooden worktops are illuminated from above in this practical line-up of appliances. Notice how there is space allocated for each task: first, the food preparation area, then the stainless steel hob and lidded deep-fat fryer, followed by an area for stacking the dishes before washing them up in the spacious sink. Below the worktop is an array of good labour-saving appliances.*

1

2

3

2 *There is an orderly marshalling of light sources in these flamboyantly shaped light bulbs, which are fitted simply in rows along the high glossy painted ceiling without shields, shades or protectors. A false ceiling has been lowered over the kitchen area to bring the light source nearer to the worktops. The use of glossy paint on the ceiling and high-gloss varnish on the teak worktop on the central island all help to catch and reflect the light. There are areas of dark, from the terracotta floor to the wooden shelves and island, which are contrasted by the white kitchen units. The mosaic made up from pieces of broken tile in primary colours on white makes an interesting splashback that is easy to reproduce at home.*

3 *This stylish kitchen contrasts dark matt blue units with chrome rails for the cook's equipment and with the stainless steel sink. Since the ceiling is lower, and in interesting stepped levels, it is painted white. Downlighters are suspended from it at strategic points to throw light on the blue. These lights have the same shape as the spotlights attached to the wall.*

Many people prefer to make the kitchen the centre of the house where the family congregate and enjoy casual meals and friendly entertaining. Increasingly, homes are designed or converted so that a dining area is provided adjacent to the kitchen rather than in a separate dining room. It is practical for the cook and washer-up as well as indicative of a change in the way we live, with less demand for formal rooms. With good planning, careful lighting and adequate ventilation, eating in or beside the kitchen need not mean eating amidst the debris and smells of food preparation.

If possible, screen off the food preparation or cooking area from the dining section. Create a lay-out which incorporates a divider in the form of an island which extends into the room and contains cupboards and a work surface or breakfast bar or a form of screen. It is sometimes possible in a smaller area to have a built-in screen which hides clutter behind a blind or doors.

Properly planned lighting which uses the correct type of fittings can be extremely effective in highlighting eating areas and dimming the food preparation area when necessary. It is essential to have dimmer switches for the flexibility they offer in a room with two separate functions – working and relaxing. Make sure you have two circuits so that each area can be separately controlled.

Spotlights are particularly effective in kitchens for highlighting specific areas. Low-voltage tungsten halogen spotlights give intense beams of light and provide a particularly attractive form of illumination, both in terms of the light they give and the style of the fitting. Small fittings or strip lights can be hidden below units. Fluorescent tubes create a cold, unattractive light but are economical. A good alternative is a tungsten strip light. Adjustable-height pendant lights for placing directly over a table are available in a wide range of styles. Whatever you choose, plan for flexibility.

Space will determine the lay-out of the kitchen/diner. People seated round a table take up a lot of space so allow plenty of room. Consider also the ease of serving food and removing dirty plates and place the table where it will not hinder a passageway. An advantage of a dining table in the kitchen is that it can double as a surface for food preparation or for another purpose such as a desk area for work or study.

Kitchen dining furniture, unlike the fine polished table and matching chairs of a formal dining room, needs to be easily washable and sturdy. Elaborate shapes, complicated mouldings or delicate finishes will be difficult to maintain in a busy, greasy kitchen environment. Also remember that the style of the table and chairs should be in keeping with that of the kitchen units. Although it may not be possible to match worktop or door surfaces exactly, choose furniture to harmonize with the kitchen decor.

A separate dining room may be
maintained in large houses, but
most homes today combine
the dining area with another
room: either it is part of the
living room or it is an extension
of the kitchen. This delightful
kitchen/dining area is divided
by a peninsular unit with an
elaborate roofing structure.
This creates an open, informal
atmosphere where the cook is
not isolated from the guests,
but where diners do not have
to look at the aftermath of food
preparation while eating. The
marble-topped cast-iron Art
Nouveau table is pushed
against this partition so that the
alcove created beside the
chimney-breast leaves room
for a chair to be pushed back.
Above the open brick fireplace,
bookshelves and an abstract
modern painting with bright
splashes of colour create a
casually charming area, while
the fire burning in the hearth
adds a comforting glow.

1 *The bay windows in this kitchen/diner suggested a shape for the working peninsula which separates the cooking from the associated dining area. Floor units with appliances and sink are grouped to form a U-shaped curve which makes full use of corner space. The outward-facing side of the peninsula has been tiled in an attractive fresh blue and white chequerboard pattern, which is easy to mop clean of any spills which occur while handing food over the counter. Once the food has been prepared, the worktop acts as a natural serving counter.*

2 *Nowhere is the principle of lighting the dining area separately from the cooking and food preparation area better illustrated than with this divided room. The kitchen, with its cool line-up of long vertical cupboards and granite worktops, is illuminated by a circular ceiling light whose bright light is useful when working. The dining area is given a different, more atmospheric treatment, with an overhead pendant light whose white shade casts a diffused light upon the round beech dining table.*

1

2

3

3 *In a small space, a central island unit can be as important for casual meals as it is for food preparation. Here, a slatted false ceiling is suspended above a beech table to define a combination work area and dining area.*

4 *Sometimes, as here, a dining table can add a sculptural and architectural grace to a kitchen. It would clearly be a mistake to spoil the main feature of the dining area – the full-length window – by blocking it with a table and chairs. The slender dining counter, with a matching shelf seemingly suspended from the ceiling, creates a natural barrier and makes the window even more of a feature. The worktop nearby provides an efficient base for serving plates and tableware.*

1 *The severe restraint of this kitchen and separate dining area makes a bold architectural statement. The kitchen is still visible, seen through the big windows framed in stained wood. The dining area has a sculptural quality, with its large square white table mounted on a black plinth and black lacquered folding chairs set against white tiles. The table is cleverly laid so as to enhance the geometry of the room and its furniture. Curved oval black place mats reproduce the cut-out shape of the chairs' backrests. The dramatically angled form of the lighting fixture over the dining room table is appropriately unfussy and modern.*

Although this kitchen/dining area began as two separate rooms, the installation of interior windows in the wall between them makes each room seem larger. An arrangement such as this would suit someone who likes to escape from the kitchen when dining, but who prefers a less formal setting than the traditional dining room.

2 *Plants make good room dividers, and work quite well when separating a kitchen and dining room so long as they are stable enough to permit access without being knocked over. Uplighters concealed at the base of tubs holding vertically growing houseplants, such as the weeping fig* (Ficus benjamina), *can cast a dappled light on the ceiling, as though you were picnicking in an indoor forest. Here, a conservatory-like indoor dining area has been created with a skylight, windows and glass doors. The kitchen, with its cool marbled worktop and white drawer units, can be seen from all sides. Lemons in hanging supermarket sacks and fruit in hanging baskets make an attractive link between the two areas. The floor is made from vinyl sheeting, which is more practical than tiles when carrying china and glass back and forth, and easy to keep clean, even when watering the numerous houseplants which decorate the area.*

DINING ROOMS

Dining rooms are disappearing with the advent of open-plan living. When space is limited it is often the first room to be sacrificed for the sake of an extra bedroom, guest room or study. Yet there is a nostalgia for that once elegant and formal setting for dinner parties and family meals. Sideboards are back. The newest kitchens include units angled and shaped like sideboards and set upon recessed plinths which perform the traditional sideboard function of storing glass, china and cutlery. The flat counter is the place for carving meat, keeping condiments and displaying salads, desserts, fruit and cheese – a feast for the eyes and the palate.

Dining tables can be truly elegant and beautiful pieces of furniture and the latest designer versions are particularly attractive. Designers have long sought to create the perfect dining chair to accompany them and as a result the choice is wide. There are Bauhaus-style chrome chairs with wicker or leather seats, shapely bentwood forms seen in restaurants, spindly black lacquer designs, simple pine and types with many other finishes, including paint and upholstery. Finally, you may wish to add a free-standing sideboard for storage.

You may prefer, or find it more economical, to search for old pieces in antique shops if you want a room with the style of a bygone age. Ensure that the accessories in the dining room are chosen to combine with the dining suite in terms of style. This can be carried through to your choice of china, glasses, condiments, place mats, serving dishes and cutlery. Creating an attractive table setting for a meal is a pleasure in itself.

Lighting should be planned to highlight the table. Unless it is a pendant which directs light on to the table, a central light will not provide a good atmosphere. Attach a dimmer to the switch for greater flexibility and use candles to create the perfect atmosphere for a special occasion.

The window in a dining room is important for daytime meals. If it provides a good view, then do not obscure it with fussy festoons or heavy curtains, which will also keep out welcome natural light. Your dining room can double as a study or home office provided you ensure there is adequate storage for equipment and papers so they can be hidden with ease before a meal.

PLANNING CHECKLIST

- How many people usually eat in your dining area?
- Do children take their meals there?
- Which meals are usually taken in the dining area?
- Do you only use the dining area infrequently or for special meals?
- Could you eat elsewhere?
- Do you wish to eat outdoors?
- Is the room used for other activities?
- Can the dining area be extended to serve a larger number of people?
- Is it easy to move between the kitchen and the dining area with food, cutlery and dishes?
- Do you wish to store tableware and cutlery in the dining area?
- What other items must be stored in the room?
- Is the dining area used most during daytime or at night? Or both?
- Do you need to be able to switch between bright task lighting and more atmospheric lighting? *Consider installing lights on a dimmer switch.*
- What atmosphere do you wish to create in the dining area?
- How much are you able to spend?

Those fortunate to find enough space for a separate dining room can create a peaceful, relaxing haven where it is possible to sit and eat and talk with friends and family. Dining room decorations do not have to be ornate or terribly formal. This restrained room is lit with a comforting glow.

1 *The furniture of a dedicated dining room generally differs greatly from that of a combination kitchen/diner. When the dining area competes with food preparation and storage for space, chairs — and even tables — may fold up for storage when not in use. Tabletops, which are likely to be pressed into service as work areas, need to be as tough and as durable as worktops. In a dining room, however, the furniture is more solid and purposeful. Honest lines, good craftsmanship and unpretentious solid oak give this dining table and six chairs a certain dignity expressive of old-fashioned values. In this dining room, one would expect to be served hearty, tasty home cooking in generous helpings, rather than artfully arranged Japanese-style or nouvelle cuisine delicacies. The rich colours of the rug, created by vegetable dyes, complement the mellow wooden furniture. The atmosphere of familiar warmth is reinforced by the alcove bookshelves, with their decoy duck, plain bowl and books, and by the bold abstract painting on the wall.*

1

2

3

2 *A craftsman was commissioned to produce this marquetry tabletop, made from blond beech inlaid with teak. Its richly patterned surface calls for extremely plain tableware and glasses of the sort visible through the glass-fronted cupboard doors. All other surfaces and finishes in the room are natural and unpretentious: exposed timber roof beams, sisal flooring, basket chairs, solid wood cupboards, a collection of wicker baskets and a gallery of framed botanical prints. The simple and unassuming decor relies on the single stunning tabletop to make a bold decorative statement.*

3 *In this long, narrow dining room, it was essential to find a table of the right shape and team it with a sideboard. A round table in this setting would leave awkward spaces at either end of the room. A glass-topped table was selected which would seem as light and as airy as possible. An ordinary wooden table would only have emphasized the shape of the room. The room is simply decorated, with great precision and an eye for geometry. Modern Italian chairs are gracefully slender.*

1 *You do not need to acquire yet another bulky piece of furniture if you want the storage and decorative benefits of a dining room dresser. You can create your own in a chimney alcove or, as here, by mounting wooden shelves above a chest of drawers. These have been given a specialist paint finish with combed colour on the carcass and sponged swirls of turquoise and white on the drawer fronts, which makes a pretty, dappled background. The wall behind is painted lemon yellow to provide a sunny complement to the blue and white china plates and platters displayed on the shelves. Jugs of fresh flowers and the weathered wood of a farmhouse table reinforce the country house look of this decor. Never be tempted to refinish a battered table top such as this. The warm patina it has developed over the years would be destroyed, and a bright finish on the newly sanded wood would only highlight surface irregularities which are difficult to remove without skilled planing.*

1

2

3

2 *It makes sense to store tableware and glasses in the dining room when possible. There has been a recent revival of interest in the traditional dining room sideboard, a piece of furniture purpose-built for storing tableware that looks as good in its setting as the table and chairs. In more casual dining rooms, dressers can perform the same function. A dresser can be decorated with a handsome china collection to create a still life which is as functional as it is pretty. Here, a round dining table, which can be more difficult to place than a rectangular one, and four traditional chairs are set against a wall that partly screens the friendly little kitchen glimpsed beyond, leaving the opposite wall for storage. Rather than install shelves which would detract from the charm of the furniture, a traditional dresser has been mixed with a line of bookshelves above to house tableware, glasses and drinks.*

3 *A little sideboard with a protected dresser top and shelves supported on ornate brackets creates a small still life. The top, lined with a marble slab, throws the collection stored on the shelves, which includes everything from decanters to old-fashioned white ceramic storage jars, into relief. Hunting in antique markets often unearths useful kitchenware bargains.*

1 *The lighting requirements for a
combination kitchen/diner can
differ greatly from those of a
separate dining room. When a
free-standing dining table is
part of a large kitchen, it helps
to have kitchen lighting
controlled by a dimmer switch
independent of the dining table
lighting. At mealtimes, kitchen
lights can be dimmed so that
clutter created while cooking
recedes into a shadowy
background, as only the dining
table is brightly illuminated.
Sometimes an overhead light
hanging from the ceiling is a
nuisance in a busy kitchen/
diner, where it is an obstacle to
be avoided. In a separate dining
room, a pendant light can hang
low over the table without
obstructing vision or traffic
flows through the room. In this
dining room, a skylight provides
lots of natural light by day, while
the two decorative pendant
lights hung at different heights
throw their pools of light upon
the table. Two wall washers
which direct light on to the pink
walls create a rosy glow of
illumination. The patterned
oilskin table cloth catches the
light and glows in warm earthy
terracotta colours. Light which
streams in through the skylight
is reflected back upwards by
the white ceramic tile floor,
making this dining room even
brighter by day.*

1

2

2 *This room reverses the balance of light and shade seen opposite. Here, warm brown cork tile flooring and a wooden table firmly anchor the room in mellow natural tones. The ice-cream pastels used elsewhere in the room — from the cream-coloured walls to the pink or white outlines painted on the woodwork, to the very pale pink blind — lighten the backdrop. The lighting for the room is all supplied by downlighters. A swivelling recessed eyeball downlighter pours a ring of light down the column which separates the dining room from the living room. Above the table is a modern Italian pendant light fitting hung on chains, with an opaque semicircular globe of light reflected in the metallic shade. Reflectors are often fitted to shield the naked bulb and can change the intensity and quality of light. Spotlights have golden reflectors built into the bulb for a warm light, or silver ones for a more mysterious light. Even on the traditional light fitting, the paper or silk shade acts as a reflector, and deflector, of the light source. Consider the change in a room's atmosphere if you were to shield the lamps with red silk, rather than white paper.*

INDEX

Page numbers in *italic* refer to
illustrations and captions

ACKNOWLEDGEMENTS

The publisher thanks the following organizations and photographers for their kind permission to reproduce the photographs in this book:

Berrymagicoal **21** *4*; Bosch **8** *1* (and plan), **9** *2* (and plan), **19** *3*, **34** *3*, **35** *5*, **54** *4*; Guy Bouchet **75** *3*; Bulthaup **21** *3*, **25** *5*, **29** *6* and *7*, **35** *7*, **38** *4*, **45** *2*, **47** *2*, **53** *3*, **54** *1*, *3* and *5*, **67** *1*; Camera Press **15** *2*, **22** *3*, **24** *1*, **25** *4*, **34** *4*, **46** *1*, **50-1** *3*; Gilles de Chabaneix **16-17**, **76**; floor by Sheppard Day Designs **50** *2*; Divertimenti **29** *5*; Eigen Huis & Interieur/Guus Rijven **1**; Elon Tiles **28** *1*, **61** *4*; Goldreif Kitchens **38** *1*, *2* and *3*; Good Housekeeping (Jan Baldwin) **21** *2*, **72-3** *1*, **74-5** *1* (David Brittain) **26** *1*, **33** *2* (John Cook) **45** *3* (Dennis Stone) **52-3** *1*; Kari Haavisto **66** *2*; Habitat **6** *1*, **6-7** *2*, **11** *2*, **48-9** *1*, **58-9** *3*, **60** *1* and *2*, **61** *3* and *5*; Kingswood Kitchens **29** *4*; Läger Kitchens **41** *5*; John Lewis of Hungerford **39** *5*; Maison Française (Philippe Leroy) **36** *1*; La Maison de Marie Claire (Pataut/Bayle) **4-5**, **62-3** *1*, **64-5** (Korniloff/Hirsch-Marie) **11** *3* (Dirand/Chauvel) **14-15** *1* (Pataut/Ardouin) **23** *4* (Pataut/Postic) **30-1** (Bouchet/Ardouin) **49** *3* (Dirand/Comte) **58** *1* (Rozès/Hirsch-Marie) **68** *1* (Pataut/Lautier) **73** *2* (Pataut/Puech) **73** *3*; Miele **28** *2*, **34** *1*, **40-1** *1*, **41** *2* and *4*; Neff (UK) Ltd (photography by David Brittain) **28** *3*, **32-3** *1*, **37** *2* and *3*, **47** *3*, **53** *2*; Plastiglide Products **55** *6*, *7* and *8*; Michael Reed (photographer Etienne Bol) **42-3**; Ianthe Ruthven **68-9** *2*; SieMatic UK Ltd **22** *1* and *2*, **24** *3*, **25** *6*, **35** *6* and *8*, **41** *3*, **50** *1*, **54** *2*, **66** *3*; Thorn EMI Major Appliances Ltd **19** *4*; Elizabeth Whiting & Associates (Jon Bouchier) **33** *3* (*Michael Dunne*) **63** *2*, **75** *2*, **77** *1* (Michael Nicholson) **11** *4*, **15** *3* (Home Improvement) **12** *1* (Neil Lorimer) **12-13** *3*, **24** *2*, **63** *3*, **66** *3* (Spike Powell) **10-11** *1*, **12** *2*, **19** *2*, **49** *2* (Tim Street-Porter) **20** *1*, **27** *2*, **56-7**; Woodstock **44** *1*; Wrighton International **34** *2*.

The following photographs were taken especially for Conran Octopus:
Simon Brown (architect Shay Cleary) **62-3**, **70-1** (architect Ian Hutchinson) **77**; Ken Kirkwood **58** *2*; Peter Mackertich **18** *1*.

Source material for the following illustrations was supplied by Homebase:
23, **29**, **45**, **47**, **60-1**